YOU ON THE MOORS NOW

BY JACLYN BACKHAUS

DRAMATISTS
PLAY SERVICE
INC.

YOU ON THE MOORS NOW was originally developed with John Kurzynowski and Theater Reconstruction Ensemble at HERE Arts Center (Reed Whitney, Producing Director), New York City, in February 2015. It was conceived and directed by John Kurzynowski, the scenic and costume design was by Joseph Wolfslau, the sound design was by Alex Hawthorn, the lighting design was by Marika Kent, and the producion stage manager was Kristy Bodall. The cast was as follows:

ELIZABETH BENNET .... Kelly Rogers
JO MARCH .... Lauren Swan-Potras
CATHY .... Anastasia Olowin
JANE EYRE .... Sam Corbin
FITZWILLIAM DARCY .... Preston Martin
LAURIE LAURENCE .... Nathaniel Basch-Gould
HEATHCLIFF .... Harlan J. Alford
MR. ROCHESTER .... Jon Riddleberger
PLAYER 1 .... Lena Hudson
PLAYER 2 .... Michael Barringer
PLAYER 3 .... Emily Marro
PLAYER 4 .... Eben Hoffer
PLAYER 5 .... Patrick Scheid
PLAYER 6 .... Claire Rothrock

ACKNOWLEDGMENTS

The script of *You on the Moors Now* that you hold in your hand is a labor of love and a meeting of minds. Theater Reconstruction Ensemble, my first artistic home in the city, was a devising company helmed by John Kurzynowski—I was their resident playwright for a time, and I crafted texts for their theatrical endeavors on several occasions. The idea to delve into these great 19th-century novels was one that John approached me about, and I was excited to explore them and mine them for content that could become a play. Over the course of several workshops, TRE actors and associated artists mined the source materials for common ground and found our angle into these disparate stories. We held an elegant ball in a rehearsal studio, we devised movement sequences and new scenarios involving our favorite characters, and we crafted several different frameworks for the piece. We performed excerpts from the piece, some that survived revisions and expansions and some that did not, at places like the Brick, HERE's Dorothy B. Williams Theater, and Fresh Ground Pepper. Eventually I was able to take these various inspirations, conversations, and teambuilt works and compile them into this play. John continually acted as a sounding board for this text as director as well as dramaturg, and the ensemble of TRE as well as Reed Whitney, TRE's producing director, were able to continually help me shape it as we readied the piece for production at HERE. The *You on the Moors Now* process felt as much an act of gathering as it did an act of writing, and so I honor those who took part in all of the work's devised genesis here.

I thank now the original cast and design team of *You on the Moors Now*, many of whom were involved in several early workshops: John Kurzynowski (director), Kristy Bodall (SM), Joseph Wolfslau (scenic, costumes), Marika Kent (lighting), Alex Hawthorn (sound), and cast: Kelly Rogers, Lauren Swan-Potras, Anastasia Olowin, Sam Corbin, Preston Martin, Nathaniel Basch-Gould, Harlan J. Alford, Jon Riddleberger, Lena Hudson, Michael Barringer, Emily Marro, Eben Hoffer, Patrick Scheid, and Claire Rothrock.

I also thank the other participants of YOTMN workshops: Nick Smerkanich, Sydney Matthews, Ben Otto, Jessie Barr, Reed Whitney, Keenan Jolliff, Mac V. Wallach, Kristine Haruna Lee, Josh Isaacs, Dylan Lamb, Libby Ricardo.

Further artistic development of the play was done with the Hypocrites in Chicago. I thank them. The team there was: Devon de Mayo (director), Justine Palmisano (SM), Arnel Sancianco (scenic), Izumi Inaba (costume), Heather Gilbert (lighting), Sarah Espinoza (sound), Shannon O'Neill (fight choreography), and Phoebe Gonzalez (dramaturg), and cast: Japhet Balaban, Maurice Demus, Tien Doman, Emjoy Gavino, Desmond Gray, Deanna Myers, Josh Odor, Brittney Love Smith, Chris Acevedo, Breon Arzell, Cruz Gonzalez-Cadel, Edward Mawere, Sarah Price, and Sarai Rodriguez.

Finally, to my agent Derek Zasky, my publishers and editors at DPS (Haleh Roshan Stilwell), and to my community of collaborators and artistic peers: Thank you for the time, the patience, the space, and the generosity of spirit you bring to our collective process.

John Kurzynowski, thank you for believing in me first.

CHARACTERS

the four women

ELIZABETH BENNET
JO MARCH
CATHY
JANE EYRE

the four men

FITZWILLIAM DARCY
LAURIE LAURENCE
HEATHCLIFF
MR. ROCHESTER

six other players play

player 1 (f)
CAROLINE BINGLEY, AMY

player 2 (m)
MR. BINGLEY, OLD MR. LAURENCE FROM NEXT DOOR

player 3 (f)
NELLY DEAN, BETH, JANE BENNET

player 4 (m)
JOSEPH, MRS. MARCH

player 5 (m)
ST. JOHN RIVERS, BHAER, EDGAR LINTON

player 6 (f)
RIVER SISTER, MEG

SETTINGS

The moors
an intersection between girlhood and womanhood
forest encampments, drawing rooms, and ballrooms across time

NOTES

Script may live on page different than on stage! Have the most fun with whatever this means.

Sections with text that is blank ("________") should be performed as though there is an implied word, name, or phrase that is too dangerous to communicate out loud. Therefore, it is communicated by ESP to those who need to know it.

Sometimes character names, scene titles, stage directions, book titles, and authors can be evoked throughout the piece (for example, at the top of scenes, or as a solution to impossibility), at the production's discretion.

This play takes characters and scenarios from *Jane Eyre* by Charlotte Brontë, *Little Women* by Louisa May Alcott, *Pride and Prejudice* by Jane Austen, and *Wuthering Heights* by Emily Brontë. You may invoke the names of these authors and these books if you need to in design, dramaturgy, and, if/when using stage directions as text, in performance.

In Act Four, the actor playing Cathy acts as narrator, taking all of the narrative text. Any dialogue should be spoken by the actor playing the corresponding character. The six players can play museum workers—hang decorations, stir punch…

YOU ON THE MOORS NOW

ACT ONE
"GIRLS STANDING ON LAWNS"

1. Moor Parkour

Soft grasses.
The sound of panting
A breeze washes over a ravine and shudders the blades of grass
A girl, running.
Tripping, falling, up again
Bounding over land
Wearing large cloaks
She seems to be fleeing something
But there is nothing behind or ahead of her
Only grasses
And rocks
And wind
And then, a second panting
Another girl joins the first girl
And they run, together
But not really together, they are of separate worlds
Sameness and separateness in their running
This second girl seems not to flee anything
Rather, she seems intent on running
As though she were proving something to the wind
She laughs with glee
And a third girl joins the second and the first
They run,
Grass, and wind, and rock
Only this girl, she runs, seemingly, through a city street

Winding past crowds, dodging carts and carriages
In the rain
And then a fourth girl
Who does not run
She merely walks
She regards the mud
She regards the weather
She walks somewhere resolutely
There is a point of focus just beyond her sight
And the other three continue to run
The four of them, there
Together, and apart
And they run
And they walk
There
On the moors
Now.

2. Jane stops. She catches her breath. She turns to the other girls.

JANE. I said no.
Did you say no?

JO. I said no.
Did you say no?

ELIZABETH. I said no.
Did you say no?

CATHY. I didn't say anything.
No one asked me anything.
I just like running.

JO. You aren't running away from anything?

CATHY. No. Are you?

JO. I was just proposed to by my neighbor

ELIZABETH and JANE. Me too
But not my neighbor

ELIZABETH. My neighbor's rich guy friend JANE. My Boss

ELIZABETH and JANE. I said no
Yeah me too

CATHY. Oh! So was I. I was just proposed to by my neighbor

ELIZABETH. What did you say?

CATHY. Nothing yet. I ran away from him

JANE. THAT'S WHAT I DID
I said no with my mind.
So you were running away from something

CATHY. No. I was just running home. It wasn't that complicated
I like to run so I ran
Because it was windy and it felt like flying.
Where are you going?

JO. I'm going home.
Which is awkward
Because we had to walk on the SAME TRAIL
From the woods where he proposed back to our cul-de-sac
And his bedroom window looks RIGHT INTO OUR HOUSE
And nobody said anything and it was just…BBLHEHBLBLBBHE-ARRGGHH
I won't see him for a while and he'll forget all about me
Where are you going?

ELIZABETH. I am going to bed
But it's not my bed
It's a hide-a-bed
I'm visiting friends.
I thought I would be safe here, but then…He showed up.
I want to go to bed.
I want to go home.

JANE. I can't go home
I don't have a home
I am literally going to run over these hills
Until I die—

ELIZABETH. It is strange, how one singular choice
Can alter the course of your life—

JANE. —Or am picked up by a wayward lady
Who drops me off at an inn
But I have no money
And I am nameless
So the inn will not take me

JO. You don't have a name?

JANE. My name is ___________

JO. I would let you stay at my house
It's kind of small but you know

JANE. Is it nearby?

JO. It's in America

JANE. Well thanks anyway

CATHY. I live nearby

ELIZABETH. Maybe you can take ___________ with you

CATHY. I can't. Sorry.
We have large dogs. And ghosts?

JANE. I HATE GHOSTS
I'll be fine
I'll venture onward
By
Myself

ELIZABETH. The life we've come from.
The life we move toward.
I'm sorry that we are unable to help you.

JANE. Help me?
Sorry for me?
No. You mustn't be sorry for me
You must be sorry for your own self
We must be sorry for our own selves
And sorry for no more than a minute
And after that, we must continue to survive
It's hard to feel sorry for yourself and survive at the same time
And I daresay, no one will do either for us.
We must do it for ourselves.

JO. If we had said yes, it would've been awful.

ELIZABETH. It would have been awful
Yes. You're right. That's why we said no.

CATHY. I might say yes. I don't know.

ELIZABETH. Do you love him?

CATHY. No, but he's rich.

JANE. UGH. I'M sorry
If I think about it—I just. I can't.
I gotta go. Bye.

Jane parkours away from them.

ELIZABETH. Wait! Are you sure you'll be alright!

JANE. *(Far away.)* No!

ELIZABETH. Godspeed, ___________.

JO. We're all fucked.

3. "Laurie"

JO. I first met Laurie behind that curtain at that rich people party.
He tried to kiss me but I had given myself a cootie shot
So I was immune.
And then we grew and grew and grew
And my sisters grew and grew
And my parents grew older and older
And then I blinked
And then I blinked and we were 18
And we went hiking
And he was acting so queer, so part of me knew it was coming and that's how I said no

A forest behind the houses.

LAURIE. Hey Jo. Wait up, will ya?
Hey, stop.
Stop right there. I gotta
I gotta talk to you about something.

JO. No, Teddy! Please! Don't do it!

LAURIE. Don't do what?

JO. Don't do that?

LAURIE. I gotta, Jo. I gotta.

JO. UGH Okay

LAURIE. So here's the thing, bitch

JO. ! I'll punch you

LAURIE. I know I'm kidding, that's like the worst way to start this

JO. HURRY UP

LAURIE. Okay hear me out
hear me out hear me out
hear me out hear me out
hear me out hear me out
hear me out.

JO. WHAT

LAURIE. I love you

JO. OH MY GOD

LAURIE. I LOVE. You. I've loved you ever since I've known you, like the first day

JO. The first day?

LAURIE. Since you hid behind that curtain

JO. SHUT UP

LAURIE. YOU SHUT UP! I've tried to tell you and show you that I love you but you wouldn't let me

JO. I wonder why

LAURIE. I decided yesterday when I saw you after I got out of my carriage that I HAD to tell you and on THIS HIKE, that I would make you listen to me because I can't go on any longer

JO. I wanted to spare you this because...I thought you understood that I—

LAURIE. Girls are so queer! You never know what they mean

JO. SHUT! UP!

LAURIE. They say no when they mean yes, and drive a man out of his wits just for the fun of it! That's an undeniable fact!

JO. I would've never hung out with you if it meant you'd think that

LAURIE. Whatever you did, I only loved you all the more for it. I worked hard to please you but in the end I was always sure I wouldn't be half good enough—

JO. No. No. I'm not half good enough for you

LAURIE. Whaddya mean JO?

JO. You're a great deal too good for me, and I'm so grateful to you, and so proud and fond of you, I don't know why I can't love you as you want me to. I've tried, but I can't change the feeling. Whatever is happening inside of me, it's telling me something clear and that clearness is the fact that I just don't love you and never will.

A silence. A wind blows through the forest.

LAURIE. Really, truly Jo?

JO. Really, truly, Laurie dear.

LAURIE. I will never love another soul. NEVER. NEVER!

Laurie stomps his foot into the ground. A quake.

JO. Um. So we should hike back now? I gotta get back to my sisters.

LAURIE. Yeah

JO. Okay. Yeah. Okay.

4. "Darcy"

Elizabeth and Darcy on the path near the trellises in the garden at Rosings Park.

ELIZABETH. I was walking, and the air was growing cold
But it was still light out
So I was trying to walk in the sunny parts of the path and avoid the shady parts
And then all of a sudden I turned around, and Mr. Darcy was there
And I can't remember what he said, at first
But all of a sudden, I found myself in the midst of it—

DARCY. In vain I have struggled—to accept the inferiority of your circumstance, but my feelings will not be repressed. You must allow me to tell you the ardence with which I admire and love you

ELIZABETH. Ardence is not a word.

DARCY. I knew it, I knew it as soon as I said it

ELIZABETH. You love me? Ardently, you say?

DARCY. I've already said it, I don't know why you need me to say it again

ELIZABETH. I will need you to say it again. I will need you to say it a few more times.

DARCY. Did you not hear me clearly the first time?

ELIZABETH. Oh, I heard you very clearly. I heard your remarks on my inferiority of birth and circumstance very clearly. I heard you say you liked me against your reason. Did you lose a bet trying to prevent this great malfeasance? *(Aside.)* Malfeasance? *(Aloud.)* Malfeasance. See a therapist? Lose a bit of sleep?

DARCY. This is not going the way it was supposed to—

ELIZABETH. Thank you for telling me, certainly. It's been such a comfort someone can be SO DRAWN to me for my "qualities" "in spite of " my "character." So thanks, and A BIG OLE
FUCK
YOU

DARCY. May I endeavour to enquire as to why with so little attempt at empathy I am to be rejected? Are you a sociopath or something?

ELIZABETH. You are a rude dickbag. BUT THAT IS NOTHING compared to my following thing which I have to say to you but I've skirted around it during this whole stupid trip to Rosings Park and so I am going to bring it up now because it is relevant and I have your audience captive: Do you think your grand parade of affection could assuage the particular grievance you have committed in separating forever my sister from perhaps her only chance at happiness?

Darcy changes colours.

Do you deny it?
Do you deny robbing my sister Jane of a chance at love?
Did you know Jane was in London?
Did you know Jane is a very shy person who has trouble expressing her feelings?
Do you deny that their separation was enacted by your hand?

Did you entice other parties i.e. Mister Charles Bingley into your line of thinking merely by suggesting your own thoughts and then coordinating his flight out of the country before anyone had a fair chance at challenging them?
Do you deny ruining her chances forever? Do you deny it?

.

.

.

And he said he could not deny it.
And then I can't remember what he said
And then it was over.
I will go to bed

5. "Heathcliff"

CATHY. I could see Heathcliff from the top of the hill
As I was running back to Wuthering Heights
He was out in the front yard chopping wood very violently
So I decided to wait to tell him about Edgar Linton until
After we'd eaten—

HEATHCLIFF. *(Interrupting.)* Cathy

CATHY. —Our supper.
Hey

HEATHCLIFF. Get inside

CATHY. Tone of voice

HEATHCLIFF. Don't just splay there like all's well

CATHY. I'm not splaying like that, I know everything in our lives is horrible
You're being rude

HEATHCLIFF. I'm always rude

CATHY. Not to me

HEATHCLIFF. What about when I threw that goat out the attic window

CATHY. That wasn't rude. That was rude to the goat, not to me

HEATHCLIFF. Just go on, huh? Go put rocks in Joseph's shoes, just get out of here

CATHY. What is wrong with you?

HEATHCLIFF. I know about Edgar Linton

CATHY. What about Edgar Linton?

HEATHCLIFF. I followed you to Thrushcross Grange and I spied on you two in the garden

CATHY. Did you hear what I said to him?

HEATHCLIFF. I left before you said yes. It was too pathetic to watch

CATHY. I didn't say yes, though, I didn't say anything

HEATHCLIFF. Stop fuckin with me, Cathy

CATHY. I didn't I didn't say yes I didn't say anything I didn't say I said I'd answer him tomorrow

HEATHCLIFF. Oh yeah?

CATHY. Yeah

HEATHCLIFF. Why'd you do that? You gotta think long and hard about it?

CATHY. Yeah

HEATHCLIFF. Lemme give ya some advice Cathy
Go and marry Edgar Linton
'Cause if you say yes to him
You're sayin no to me
And that's plenty fine
Because I'm never gonna ask you anyway

CATHY. Why would I ever think you would ask me to marry you?

HEATHCLIFF. Because you're in love with me.

CATHY. You're an asshole

HEATHCLIFF. The thought of me sets you off in a frenzy. And how will you overcome it?
"If I were to marry Heathcliff, we should be beggars"

CATHY. *(Realizing.)* Who told you that? Nelly Dean? Did Nelly Dean tell you that?

HEATHCLIFF. Oh Nelly Dean told me a lot of things

CATHY. You're a pig

HEATHCLIFF. You're a bitch

CATHY. I hate you

HEATHCLIFF. I hate you too
Get inside

CATHY. And then I slapped him
And then I went inside
And I wrote a note to Edgar Linton, it said "YES"
And then I went outside with it.
Heathcliff?

HEATHCLIFF. What now?

CATHY. Can you deliver this to Thrushcross Grange?
I'll give you tuppence for your troubles.

Heathcliff takes the card. He drops the axe. He leaves. She watches him go.

I am Heathcliff
And he is me
And I cannot marry myself.

6. "Rochester"

Jane, alone, parkouring. Soldiering on, away from Thornfield.

JANE. Step, Jane
Roll, Jane
One by one, Jane
One by one

But her mind keeps wandering.
Jane and Rochester stand by a huge tree.
The tree is old and gnarled and knotted and knobbed.
It has scary limbs and branches.
There is a light from the house.
There is a slight breeze.
It is night.

ROCHESTER. Ireland. You'll like it.

JANE. *(Aside.)* Inside my head. Alarum bells.

ROCHESTER. The people. The scenery. The food. Mrs. Dionysus O'Gall. Bitternut Lodge.

JANE. It's a long—way.

ROCHESTER. From here, but what is here? This old ugly tree? This beanfield?

JANE. *(Realizing.)* Beans

ROCHESTER. A girl like you would not object to the voyage. Or the distance. A strong…constitution

JANE. I don't object to the voyage or the distance sir but, the sea is a barrier

ROCHESTER. England and Thornfield are just boops on a map you know

JANE. From you. Sir. A barrier from you

She begins to cry LARGE SOBS.

ROCHESTER. I have a strange—a FEELING. With regard to you. And I'm just like WHAT IS THIS? Stop crying there's this string going from my ribs and it's winding around my…heart? And it pulls through the back of my…spine and when you tug on it I fall over? WHAT AM I SAYING? DO YOU WANT TO LEAVE? ARE YOU SORRY TO GO?

JANE. I am sorry because at Thornfield I h-h-have lived a fruitful life. I h-h-have felt like the world needs me and I am needed in the…world. I'm not some Halfling starving to death begging for food. I'm not petrified, or quaking in my boots. I'm not afraid anymore! Did you hear that? I'm not afraid anymore! But to know that I would be torn away from you, Mr. Rochester, leaves me more anguished and terrified than I've ever been in my LIFE and I AM AN ORPHAN WHO WAS TERRORIZED BY GHOSTS AS A CHILD, because in your company I've never been h-h-h-happier!

ROCHESTER. Why would you be torn from me?

JANE. BECAUSE your WIFE

ROCHESTER. MISS INGRAM? MISS INGRAM?

JANE. MISS INGRAM! MISS INGRAM!

ROCHESTER. SHE'S NOT MY FUCKIN WIFE YET!! I HAVE *(Face.)* no wife—

JANE. I TELL YOU I MUST GO!
Do you think I can stay to become nothing to you? Do you think I am a robot? A Machine without feelings? And can bear to have my morsel of bread snatched from my lips and my drop of living water dashed from my cup? Do you think

—BECAUSE I AM POOR
—BECAUSE I AM OBSCURE
—BECAUSE I AM PLAIN
—BECAUSE I HAVE TINY HANDS

That I am SOULLESS? HEARTLESS? You think wrong! I have A SOUL AND A HEART BIGGER THAN ANY OF THOSE YOU HOST, and if God had gifted me with

—WEALTH
—BEAUTY
—ESTEEM
—LARGE HANDS

I would have made it as hard for you to leave me as it is now for me to leave YOU!

And this speech is MORTIFYING BUT ALSO GREAT BECAUSE I am not speaking from a place of custom nor of convention nor of mortal flesh. This is my spirit and your spirit. And we are equal. And BECAUSE OF THIS, I AM GOING. AND YOU CAN'T STOP ME.

ROCHESTER. WE ARE EQUAL. AS WE ARE. SO, JANE

KISS.

JANE. NO JANE
NO
STRIKE IT FROM YOUR BRAIN
JANE
STRIKE IT FROM YOUR BRAIN
SOLDIER ON
FORWARD MARCH
HUP HO
HUT TWO THREE FO

FORWARD
ONWARD
ONWARD
But what is he doing now?
What is he thinking?

ROCHESTER. You wanna know what I'm DOING right now?
This morning I turned my breakfast over
And then I threw up
And then I called your name out the window four times.
And then I cried into my bedsheets
And then I burned all of my clothes, and then your clothes
And then I rode my horse for a long time. Hyah!

Rochester gets on his horse. He rides with abandon, to no place.
The other men see what Rochester has done and join in,
Taking part in a party for Male Grief.
Next is Mr. Darcy. He pulls out a Letter he has Just Written.
He reads:

DARCY. "Be not alarmed, madam, on receiving this letter, by the apprehension of its containing any repetition of those sentiments or renewal of those offers which were last night so disgusting to you. I write without any intention of paining you, or humbling myself, by dwelling on wishes which, for the happiness of both, cannot be too soon forgotten..."

Laurie pulls out a large trunk. He is despondent
He has just returned home after Jo has rejected him.
He opens the trunk and throws pertinent traveling gear in it.

LAURIE. Fine.
If she doesn't want me
Then I DON'T WANT HER
I'LL MAKE HER RUE the day she ever walked away from
THEODORE LAURENCE
Ahhhh

He gets teary.

It ALL REMINDS ME OF HER
SHE GAVE ME THAT TENNIS RACKET
SHE MADE ME THAT FAKE PLAQUE WITH MY FACE ON IT

"WORLD'S BEST BOOGERFACE"
I'm gonna go to Europe.
I'm gonna go to Paris and East Berlin
And West Berlin and Heidelberg and Prague and Prussia
I'm gonna go to Vienna
I'm gonna eat sausage
I'm gonna be successful and marry a model
And she's gonna be NOTHING

Heathcliff paces by candlelight.

HEATHCLIFF. I am Heathcliff, blah blah blah
YOU KNOW WHAT?
FUCK WEDDINGS
I HATE EM
I'LL MARRY WHOEVER,
AND GUESS WHAT
I WON'T FUCKING GIVE TWO SHITS ABOUT IT
This is a waste of time. How long will I be alive?
The year is 18-something
I might catch a pox and die
The kinds of people who catch pox are weak
And I'm SO MUCH MORE THAN THIS PROVINCIAL LIFE
I
HAVE
HAD
ENOUGH!!!!!

The men stop grieving.

DARCY. *(Signing off real quick.)* "God Bless You, Fitzwilliam Darcy."

ELIZABETH. I can't bear it.
He sends me this letter just to—what? Prove to me that I've been wrong this whole time?
I turn him down, and what becomes of him?

JO. He gets over me,
And he goes on to prominence
While I continue to struggle my way

CATHY. He distances himself from everyone
He makes the world worse, in spite and ill spirit

ELIZABETH. He continues on his way, better than he was before
These men, they grieve,
They go riding
Or they travel
Or they ask someone else to marry them
Or they take it out on the person nearest them
Or all of the above.

JANE. The world gives them the chance to "get over it"
And we climb over hills away from them
We starve ourselves
And run away

DARCY. Do you have any idea—
Do you remember when and how I loved you?

ELIZABETH. No

DARCY/ROCHESTER/HEATHCLIFF/LAURIE. It all came rushing to me in a moment
It was the moment you…

Each of them remembers, silently, a moment when the boys loved the girls.

JO. Okay. So, is that supposed to make us change our minds?

LAURIE. Well—

HEATHCLIFF. We hardly even got a turn to speak.

CATHY. That's not our problem.

ROCHESTER. Well. That wasn't how we thought it would turn out.

JO. How did you think it would turn out?

HEATHCLIFF. I don't know. Better than this.

ELIZABETH. Yeah, well, good thing you're so confident. It'll serve you well in the life that you lead without me.

JO. Yeah, good thing you're all so sure of yourselves. It's a good thing you learned that at an early age

CATHY. Or maybe it's just an inherent part of being a man

JANE. Something men know and women are expected to deal with

ELIZABETH. And all we are asked to do is make ourselves presentable in case another prospect formulates

CATHY. It's very hard to be denied something, isn't it?

JO. Yeah, it's SOOOO HARD

JANE. Yeah!
(To the boys.) You know what?
GET OVER IT

ELIZABETH. GET OVER IT

JO. YEAH, GET OVER IT

DARCY. Hey!

HEATHCLIFF. Ow

CATHY. Think of the world. There is a bigger world. More than us, than love
and I want to TAKE IT.

JO. Why can I not travel
Why can I not ask someone to marry me?
Why must I hold it in?

ELIZABETH. My duty is to my family
My duty is to my family line

JANE. My duty is to my self
And I don't even know who I am.
SO I AM GOING TO TAKE THIS OPPORTUNITY TO LEARN ABOUT MYSELF

JO. AND WHAT I WANT

CATHY. I AM GOING TO LIVE PRESENTLY

ELIZABETH. AND THEN I WILL LOVE PRESENTLY

CATHY. THERE IS A BIGGER WORLD

JO/ELIZABETH/CATHY/JANE. AND I DESERVE IT
AND I WILL FIND IT

ELIZABETH. I must find my sisters

JO. I must find my sisters

JANE. I must find some sisters

CATHY. Sisters.

JO/ELIZABETH/CATHY/JANE. Excuse us.

ELIZABETH. We are OUTTA HERE

The girls leave.

LAURIE. We should team up or something

HEATHCLIFF. *(Eyeroll.)* Oh yeah, totally. Great idea. Where are you from

LAURIE. Like, outside Boston

HEATHCLIFF. Of course you are.

DARCY. Rochester, I don't even know what happened with you. I thought she said yes

ROCHESTER. She found out I had another wife locked up in the attic

DARCY/HEATHCLIFF/LAURIE. Ooof

ROCHESTER. She found out the day of our wedding

DARCY/HEATHCLIFF/LAURIE. OOOF
Sucks

ROCHESTER. Yeah tell me about it.

HEATHCLIFF. Well what the fuck are we gonna do?

DARCY. I don't know, man. I don't know.

LAURIE. They're all running to their sisters. That is like a Berlin Wall made of women.

DARCY.	ROCHESTER.
We are totally fucked	Let's TEAR IT DOWN.

The boys are alone.
They have no one to perform at.
They are cold, they are afraid.
Lights out.

End of Act One

a MOVEMENT PIECE shall Transition us!

Women run by while Players search with lanterns for them.

RIVER SISTER. From underneath the baseboards of each great house
Forms descend upon the landscape
Unmoored by the loss of the Missing Heroines

Men run on, Heathcliff delivers the note to Edgar Linton, and then runs off.

What of Heathcliff?
Some say he's wandering near jagged rocks and eating them
But is he, really?

Cathy comes on in a veil and walks down the aisle with Linton, the Players all bow.

What of Cathy?
It was a spring wedding
But they say the honeymoon's a coverup
and she's really somewhere else
What of the men?

The men run on again—Laurie delivers a hanky to audience members; Heathcliff whispers to Joseph; Darcy whispers to Bingley and they share a little high-five they made up; then Caroline tries to flirt with Darcy, he brushes her off.

LAURIE. Hankies out gentlemen
To anyone of assistance in our search
We will not rest until they are found
BY US

DARCY/ROCHESTER/HEATHCLIFF/LAURIE. YEAH

ROCHESTER. We will not move from this camp
until we move closer to where they are!

DARCY/ROCHESTER/HEATHCLIFF/LAURIE. YEAH

Jane runs on and collapses, River Sister and St. John pick her up and carry her off.

RIVER SISTER. Every clink of tea is suspect

Every cloaked figure is apprehended
and searched for tiny hands.
What of the women?

Lastly, the women run on again and do their high-five, realizing Jane isn't with them, and off they run.

JO. We'll be safe here
let's set up camp

ELIZABETH. Where's Jane Eyre?

CATHY. I dunno
I'll keep watch.

RIVER SISTER. They say dropped hankies are not what they seem
They say Undone ribbons are precious
There are rumblings
Rumours across the moors
of a fissure
between women and men

ACT TWO
"ALL'S FAIR IN LOVE AND MOORS"

From underneath a portal in the floorboards
From out of the ether, forms descend
Upon the boards and make their home
As they keep watch for signs of the Missing Four
From over the hills we hear a ringing.
The clinks of tea
The clinks of spoons on cups
And we see
Large swaths of cloth
With people in them
Moving, strutting,
Large sounds with every movement of cloth
We smell burning fires, and cardamom
Rosewater, and sealing wax
We feel hairpins in hair and perspiration
We see sugar melt in hot liquids
It is winter in
The Drawing Room
And the ghosts of books and large wigs and tradition loom over
Teatime conversation.

1. "Caroline and Mr. Bingley from *Pride and Prejudice* by Jane Austen sip tea at Netherfield Park."

CAROLINE. Did you hear what I asked, Mr. Bingley?
Oh brother, come now, you seem so listless!

BINGLEY. Lists? Lists?

CAROLINE. You're not even drinking your tea, brother Mr. Bingley

BINGLEY. Oh, Caroline, What good is tea? I've got so much on my mind

CAROLINE. Are you STILL thinking about that girl Jane Bennet?

BINGLEY. I am very unfortunate as to have made the decision I have made, to quit Netherfield and not further engage in my pursuit of the provincial beauty Jane Bennet!

CAROLINE. Jane Bennet didn't even like you. Darcy said so

BINGLEY. Well
there's more
Darcy went and proposed to her sister

CAROLINE. *(The beast emerges.)* WWWWWWHHHHHHAAAAAAAAAAT?!?!?!?!?!?!!!

BINGLEY. LIZZY BENNET! AND SHE! Said no.

CAROLINE. ——O——O——

BINGLEY. And then she went away and nobody knows where!
Ugh, there's so much going on
If only I had a sister like a good sisterly sister who would do her best to ask fellow ladies in her station about Lizzy Bennet's whereabouts. If ONLY I had that—
You haven't heard anything about where Lizzy Bennet went, have you? Her whereabouts? Any signs of her or the other three?

CAROLINE. I'm sorry I

Sobs.

I thought Darcy would marry me

BINGLEY. Oh dear, you can't think about that now
Is she with her mother? Did she go on a trip with her aunt and uncle? Is she traveling alone, or with others?

CAROLINE. *(Devastation.)* I THOUGHT HE WOULD MARRY ME

BINGLEY. CAROLINE. CALM YOURSELF.
If you do find anything out, about Lizzy or her Sisters, please don't be afraid to use your womanly keen to discern it for me…after all… I do so long to get in touch again with the Provincial Beauty Jane Bennet again

CAROLINE. *(Woozy.)* The Bennets…
I might hurl
Like all over the place

BINGLEY. Oh dear!
Do you need me to!

To get a bucket!
Or a!
A plastic bag!
Wait!
Can I!
Hold your hair!
Oh God!
Somebody call for help!
I'll call for help!
Help!
Here I have a hanky in my—

Bingley reaches into his pocket, and grabs a crumpled up hanky. He unfolds it, he reads. He quickly crumples it back up again.

CAROLINE. Wait what's this? *(Reading hanky.)* "Bingley—use Caroline against Lizzy Bennet—"

BINGLEY. *(Snatch it!)* What? No… what? So my hanky had words on it. Don't worry! Nothing to worry about. Not important at all.
I should throw it away.

2. "Nelly Dean and Joseph from *Wuthering Heights* by Emily Brontë clean a chimney at Wuthering Heights."

NELLY. Joseph, will ya pass me that dustpan
I want the house bright n clean fer when Miss Cathy arrives back wither new husband, Edgar Linton

JOSEPH. O YE WAN TA PAN E DOOS?
OYLL GI YA DOOS
LOR JAYSU NEER AS FOR THE DOOSPAN
HE OLLY EER FARTCHED I HISELF
YA WENCH

NELLY. you wretched man
I'll fetch it myself

She gets up and shakes her dress out. Ash and soot poof out, Joseph sneezes.

JOSEPH. A'CHOO
A'CHOO
A'CHOO
CURSE-YA NELLY

NELLY. Bless ya, Joseph
Do ya think Miss Cathy and and her new husband Edgar Linton will live here? Or Abroad?
When they return from travelin newly married like

JOSEPH. I DANOO NELLY
I DANOO.
DYA KNO
WAR is she NAW???

NELLY. I haven't half an inklin where Cathy is Joseph

JOSEPH. YASOOR ABOUT DA NELLY?

NELLY. Oh I'm sure of it Joseph.
Ya know.
Sometimes I wonder if Heathcliff is lovesick over Cathy

JOSEPH. NEVAAAAAAAAAAAA

NELLY. well she left in such a fuss and you remember the log

JOSEPH. HOW DAR YA MAKE EATCLIF LOOK LYKA WEAKLIN
WHEN IS CA--Y
ROTTEN CA--Y
WHO ROONED THIS HOUSE FAREVAAAAAAA
U KNO WAR SHE IS NAW DONTCHA

NELLY. I DON'T KNOW WHERE SHE IS NOW JOSEPH

<table>
<tr><td>JOSEPH.
WARS CA--Y
WARS CA--Y
I SHE SALIN
I SHE MOONCHIN ONA
PMAGRANAT IN SINS FER O TIME
N WARR N WARRRR N WAARRRR
SHE IDIN NELLY SHE IDIN WAR
YA CUR NELLY IDIN OUT WENCH</td><td>NELLY.
STOP ASKIN
STOP IT Joseph
Why'd she be sailin

A pomegranate. That's rude
Joseph
Hidin?
what do you mean hidin?
why do you think Cathy's
hidin?</td></tr>
</table>

IN TOIM I'LL GET THE TRUTH FROM YA
find out where she's idin
A'CHOO

Joseph sneezes, he takes out a hanky. He reads it. Nelly sees.

NELLY. Bless ya Joseph
You got some words on yer hanky there Joseph
What's it say

JOSEPH. Nevah

NELLY. God Love ya, Joseph
But yer the worst coworker I ever did have

JOSEPH. BLECH

3. "St. John and River Sister from *Jane Eyre* by Charlotte Brontë sit and do taxes in their small cottage on the Moors (now)."

RIVER SISTER. Brother St. John,* you haven't answered my question

ST. JOHN. Sorry, sister. I'm doing the taxes.

RIVER SISTER. So am I

ST. JOHN. Well… clearly you're not doing them hard enough, because you're finding time to chat me up

RIVER SISTER. I'm not chatting you up. I am literally asking you
Very urgently
If you've given any thought to the unconscious woman you picked up out of the gutter
Who is sleeping on the chaise longue in our study

ST. JOHN. Oh. "That."

RIVER SISTER. Yes, that.

ST. JOHN. I don't know? Maybe we'll figure it out when she wakes up?
It's weird because there's a lot more to think about right now
And you're making a lot of fuss about a pretty logical situation

* Pronounced "Sinjin."

RIVER SISTER. So you have the answer then?

ST. JOHN. Yeah.
I'll give her a job at the school
Or we'll get her the fuck outta here

RIVER SISTER. You're obnoxious

ST. JOHN. Deal with it. I'm goin to India soon so whatever.

RIVER SISTER. I'm done.
I'm going to check on her

River Sister leaves. She comes back.

She's gone, St. John

ST. JOHN. *What?*

RIVER SISTER. She left a note
"Thanks for the clothes."

ST. JOHN. That's all it said?

RIVER SISTER. Yup

ST. JOHN. Nothin else?

RIVER SISTER. No

ST. JOHN. Goddammit.

RIVER SISTER. What is it, St. John?

ST. JOHN. I already sent a hanky to the men's camp, telling them I had her, that's what.
She claimed to be nameless, but I saw right through it all.
She's one of the four. The one with the tiny hands.
I had Jane Eyre right HERE. And then I LOST HER.
How will I ever face them now?

RIVER SISTER. *(Suddenly grave.)* Face who, St. John?
Face who?
Face who??

4. "The March Sisters from *Little Women* by Louisa May Alcott practice their singing in Massachusetts."

MRS. MARCH. Amy…Meg…Beth…

MEG. A one, two, three, four

Amy, Meg, and Beth take on the stance of an Andrews Sisters girl group. Snapping fingers, snapping toes. Mrs. March presides.

AMY, MEG, and BETH. *(Singing.)*
Thanks for the clothes, Jo
Thanks for the clothes, Jo
You're on your own, Jo
Down in New York
Thanks for the clothes, Jo
We love them so, Jo
Thanks for the clothes, Jo
Thanks for the clothes.

Mrs. March claps!

MRS. MARCH. OH, DEARS.

AMY, MEG, and BETH. Mother!

MRS. MARCH. If only Jo could hear you now.

AMY. Did she send anything else in the parcel she sent?

MRS. MARCH. Nope.

BETH. If only I could go to New York like her!

AMY. If only Jo could travel home from New York and come to our gig on Saturday.

MEG. We have to work on the bridge

BETH. on it

AMY. Beth, are you going to be alright to perform on Saturday?

BETH. Yeah

AMY. You just seem a little tired.

BETH. I'm fine

MEG. Are you sure

MRS. MARCH. Girls! Leave Beth alone!
Beth, work on the bridge
HEY We got a letter

AMY, MEG, and BETH. Mother! Who's it from!

MRS. MARCH. Old Mr. Laurence

BETH. Can I read it?

MRS. MARCH. Sure

BETH and MR. LAURENCE. Hey there, Marches
I'm so sad to say
I will have to politely decline your invitation to hear you sing on Saturday
Down at O'Hooligans
Laurie is, uh, leaving that very day on his uh "ship out to Florence"
A Laurence in Florence is worth two in the bush.
He's been pretty DOWN IN THE DUMPS if you ask me
Don't know why
Literally have no idea what's wrong
Okay, gotta jet.
Love
Old Grandpa Laurence from Next Door

MRS. MARCH. Well, that's too bad

BETH. Jo's in New York and now Laurie's in Florence!

AMY. A Laurence in Florence.
Mother, do you think I will get to go to Florence?

MRS. MARCH. You'll go wherever the rich people tell you to go.

MEG. Should we keep practicing?

AMY. Yeah

BETH. Let's do it one last time.

MEG. And a one, and a two

MARCHES. *(Singing.)*
 Thanks for the clothes,
 Jo Thanks for the clothes,
 Jo You're on your own,
 Jo Down in New York

The girls sashay back
And back
And back
Mrs. March has a little dance, and then she drops her motherly façade and goes over to the Laurence house to meet with Mr. Laurence, who has been listening to the whole exchange from across the lawn with a big stethoscope.
It becomes clear that Mrs. March has been spying for the men's side.

MRS. MARCH. Did you hear what they said?

MR. LAURENCE. What?

MRS. MARCH. Did you hear what they said?

MR. LAURENCE. What?

MRS. MARCH. Did you hear what they said?

MR. LAURENCE. New York. They're meeting in New York.
Just Jo? Or the other ones?

MRS. MARCH. Rumor is that's the meeting spot
That's all we know for now

MR. LAURENCE. Well why don't we crash this meeting spot.
We need one of ours to nail down the coordinates

MRS. MARCH. Who can we rely on?

MR. LAURENCE. We got Bingley. Charles Bingley in London
We got the two of us.
We got that servant guy Joseph out on the moors
And we got St. John.

MRS. MARCH. We don't have anyone in New York?

MR. LAURENCE. Not a one.
We need somebody who knows them
We need somebody on the inside
And then the cogs will fall into place

MRS. MARCH. Well I know a guy. A professor. In New York. We can get him on our team.
I'll send a letter tonight.
Any word from camp?

MR. LAURENCE. What?

MRS. MARCH. I know a guy. A professor. In New York. We can get him on our team.
I'll send a letter tonight.
Any word from camp?

MR. LAURENCE. I got a hanky last week, from Laurie
He said it's he, Mr. Darcy, and Mr. Heathcliff, and Mr. Rochester
Out there, somewhere on the moors now
They've got rifles, poisons, spears, and maps
The men have encamped, now, Mrs. March
And they are ready to March
They are hunters, horsemen, Scholars
Their wits and braun will never be outmatched
and they will find
Jane Eyre. Liz Bennet. Jo March. And...Cathy
Wherever they are hiding
In whatever wood or glen they have made home
And on that day, the Seizing Day,
Men everywhere will rise up and take their posts
And pull the coverlet off this female design
And we shall be victorious
And emerge from the battle with scars on our eyelids
Scars where our hearts were
Scars in all the places where we bleed and weep for the ones we love
The ones who do not love us back
This war may not be over yet
But by God, let's see to it that we give it a loud ending
Let's see to it that the girlfolk
The women
Never turn their backs again.
Well. Let's talk soon.
Before the storm

THUNDER. LIGHTNING.
GRASSES BLOW IN WIND.
SIDEWAYS RAIN. SNOW. SNAIN.
They all run for cover.

5. "You Eating S'Mores Now."

An encampment near New York City.
Lizzy, Cathy, and Jo sit across from Edgar Linton.

CATHY. I'm afraid we all agree that you're fired
From our camp, Edgar Linton.

EDGAR. But Cathy, I'm your husband

CATHY. You don't support my wants
And you are bad with dogs, Edgar Linton.

EDGAR. But Cathy, you're my wife

CATHY. I'm also your employer
And unfortunately it's time for you to pack your things and go.

Edgar gets up. He extends a hand. Cathy shakes it. He picks up an errant canteen and perhaps one of those hitchhiker's bundles on a stick.
He leaves.

ELIZABETH. That was a lot easier than I thought it would be

JO. Good job, Cathy

A rustling.

Shhh. What was that

CATHY. On my word...grab your weapons.

They all put their hands to their waists. Jane stumbles into camp.

CATHY/ELIZABETH/JO. JANE!

JANE. I MADE IT!

They hug.

ELIZABETH. We were so worried about you!
We sent dozens of ribbons!
Dozens, but—

CATHY. We are afraid they were intercepted
By spies for

CATHY/ELIZABETH/JO. The men

JANE. They're spying?
On us?

JO. Forget about them!
You made it!
You're here! You're here
Ugh you guys!
WE'RE HERE!

They hug. It's been so long. They are excited and moved. Cathy abstains from the hug.

CATHY. I've gotta keep watch.

ELIZABETH. Jane what took you so long?

JANE. Somewhere along the road after we split up
I got sick and fainted
And I woke up in a house with these two siblings
I snagged this disguise and escaped.

CATHY. Well hey *(Sits.)*
Take a load off
We're in charge around these parts

High-fives.
Jo roasts marshmallows around a campfire.

JO. Anyone want a s'more?

CATHY. I want one

ELIZABETH. I'll have one

Jane and Lizzy and Cathy all take sticks. They roast marshmallows. They pass around graham crackers, chocolate.

CATHY/ELIZABETH/JO/JANE. Mmmm.

JANE. So what'd I miss while I was detained?

JO. We…
We got jobs

They all squeal.

JANE. WHAT
THEY LET YOU GET JOBS
WHAT KIND OF JOBS

ELIZABETH. Okay well I didn't get a job.

I started school.
I am taking Organic Chemistry
It's so. It's so hard.
I study every night for hours
It makes me feel so smart and so stupid at the same time

JO. I got a job at a local paper!

JANE. For writing?!?!?!!

JO. I proofread
I fact check
And I write
And sometimes they even let me keep my own byline

CATHY. I got hired by this boat
At first they wanted me to be a deck wench
And they wanted Edgar to be first mate
But they quickly realized Edgar is useless and I'm good at tying knots
So I took his job

JANE. Whoa.

CATHY. They pay me less than they paid him
But, you know
We've got to go at this one step at a time.
What job do you want, Jane?

JANE. I think. I want to be. In Space.

They all pause for a moment to regard the vastness and unknowability of space.

Has anyone talked to their families yet?

CATHY. No.

JO. Well Cathy you don't really have a

ELIZABETH. Shhh. Jo!

JANE. I don't either you know so
I sympathize

CATHY. Whatever it's fine
I keep watch I do my part
It's fine

JO. My sisters know roughly of our whereabouts
And, in case any trouble arises, they'll be here.

ELIZABETH. I've been sending ribbons to my sisters
Their network is growing
Slowly
But it's growing

CATHY. Lizzy's sisters have set up a resistance front
They're having meetings with all four and twenty families
And getting other women to the cause…

6. "Caroline Bingley invites Jane Bennet over for Tea."

CAROLINE. So Jane Bennet!! How are you?
Isn't it simply divine that we're both from *Pride and Prejudice* AND that we're seeing each other and we're both in London
AT THE SAME TIME?

JANE BENNET. It's quite funny, Caroline Bingley. I must say. And your brother? Mr. Bingley?

CAROLINE. OH, my brother! He's here and there when he's in town of course
But he's been

JANE BENNET. Conveniently out of the city on Business?

CAROLINE. Yes—he's—that's—how did you know that?

JANE BENNET. My sources told me you'd be alone today. Which means I can ask you what I've been meaning to ask you: Did your brother ask you to invite me to tea?

CAROLINE. Yes, but it is because he loves you—because he wanted me to ask you.—

JANE BENNET. He wanted information about Lizzy. Caroline,
You are being used as a pawn for the men's side

CAROLINE. The MEN'S SIDE! How dare you, the insolence to suggest that—

JANE BENNET. Did they promise you something?
Did they promise you Darcy in exchange for your cooperation?

CAROLINE. *(DEVASTATION.)* HE WAS SUPPOSED TO MARRY

ME
I'M RICH
I'M BEAUTIFUL
I HAVE SOCIAL GRACES

JANE. Caroline. Your brother is using you.
Darcy will not marry you for your troubles. There is no happy ending.
Have you noticed any strange hankies lying around?

CAROLINE. *(Still devastated.)* You mean the hankies with the words on them?

JANE BENNET. If you stand with us, then you will tell your brother
I was never here
And you will start reporting all of his actions to me by ribbon
Good day, Miss Bingley.

Jane exits.
A beat. Caroline composes herself.
Mr. Bingley enters.
He shakes his umbrella off.

BINGLEY. Hello, Caroline.
How was your tea with Jane Bennet?

CAROLINE. She...she...she couldn't make it after all.

BINGLEY. Damn. That's...too bad...

Bingley sneaks away, and writes a letter on his hanky.

Darcy—It's Bingley, code name Bird-dog.
The Bennets got to Caroline
She won't cooperate any longer.
Gotta jet.
Love, Bird-dog

7. "Boys Camp"

Heathcliff, Darcy, Laurie, and Rochester huddle under a blanket in the wind and snain. Heathcliff has been trying to build a fire.

ROCHESTER. We'll have to eat canned beans again

HEATHCLIFF. I'M. SICK. OF CANNED. BEANS

DARCY. IT'S CALLED ROUGHING IT. WE ARE ROUGHING IT
THIS WAS YOUR IDEA, HEATHCLIFF

HEATHCLIFF. DON'T FUCKIN START WITH ME, DARCY

ROCHESTER. Hey. GUYS
COOL IT.

LAURIE. Rain is stopping. The rain is stopping!

ROCHESTER. GOOD EYE, LAURENCE!

The rain drip, drip, drops. And stops.

HEATHCLIFF. I'm starting up the fire again.

DARCY. So what's on the menu? Fried beans?

HEATHCLIFF. I shot a peasant. A Pheasant.

ROCHESTER. Darcy, Heathcliff's gonna fry the pheasant. We are gonna talk plans. Who's got the map?

LAURIE. I do!
Shit, it's wet

DARCY/HEATHCLIFF/ROCHESTER. Aw c'mon

LAURIE. No, it's—it's only damp, okay? Okay look.

He rolls out a large map. Heathcliff fries pheasant.

ROCHESTER. Run me through this again, Laurie.

LAURIE. Here. Here
Okay. SO here's our camp.
Here's where we split off from the girls.
Here is how many miles we've traveled.
This circle is how many miles they have presumed to travel
It's not many.

DARCY. Who made these calculations?

HEATHCLIFF. I did.
I also cook the food.
You're welcome.

ROCHESTER. And correspondence? Has anyone had any new correspondence?
Last I heard from St. John Rivers, Jane escaped
But he had her
But she escaped.

DARCY. I received a hanky from Bird-dog who said
his sister Caroline Bingley is having Lizzy Bennet's sister Jane Bennet for tea.
We'll see if he gleans anything from it.

Another hanky comes for Darcy. He reads it.

Fuck. It didn't work.

LAURIE. A hanky just came in to me, too.
From my grandfather.

LAURIE and MR. LAURENCE. "Dear Laurie,
Heard from Mrs. March today.
Jo is definitely in New York. Not sure with who. Not sure whereabouts
Sent a hanky to this professor we know
But he doesn't seem very cooperative.
See if you can brainstorm any other helpers.
Love you
Eat your prunes
Love
Grampy"

HEATHCLIFF. New York falls into my calculations. So.

LAURIE. We have dispatches
Employed in each of the four households.
Anything they hear from the women
They send to us
I'm sure it's only a matter of time before
We start getting more and more specific
And we can finally start to move.

A rustling in the grass.

The men at attention.

DARCY. WHAT WAS THAT?

ROCHESTER. Men. Grab your weapons.
On my word, we fire!

A rustling. And then Edgar Linton appears.

DARCY/HEATHCLIFF/ROCHESTER/LAURIE. Edgar Linton.

EDGAR. I KNOW WHERE THEY ARE.

Intermission!

ACT THREE
"YOU IN THE WARS NOW"

The girls' camp. After work. Dinnertime. S'mores. Studying. Lizzy reads a giant Organic Chemistry textbook.

ELIZABETH. Any news from the workfront y'all?

JANE. One of the kids barfed. The space camp kids
They always barf at zero-gs

They all bite their s'mores.

JO. I ran into some trouble after work
Some German bartender was acting creepy so I had to pull a knife out.

JANE. Did you knife him?

JO. Well, I thought about it.

A flash to Jo after work.
A dimly lit barroom in lower Manhattan. A Germanic man polishes glass, rag on shoulder.
Jo stumbles in, covered in rain.

JO. Double scotch rocks

BHAER. Yaaa. Vat is your name?

JO. Jo

BHAER. Jo Vhat?

Jo pulls out a knife.

JO. Why do you wanna know, German?

BHAER. W-wait—no I didn't mean, just coss I like ze vay you order drinx so I vanted to take you out sometime zat's all nothing else no ozer reason

JO. I've heard a lot of things from a lot of people.

BHAER. My name is Bhaer I'm a grad styudent I'm a PHD candidate for vurldhistory

JO. Oh yeah?

BHAER. Ya I haff my styudent ID card somewhere in my pocket one sex I mean sec acchhh I hate English sometimes wait wait okay here it is

He shows her his ID card.

JO. Okay.

BHAER. *(Closer.)* Take my address down as collateral for your trust:
I've heard about you guys from the men
Somebody got in touch with me
To be on ze lookout for you.
But I'm on your side okay? Your side.

JO. How can I trust you?

BHAER. Drinx on ze house. Don't even tip me okay? Lay low.

He pours a little for himself. They cheers.
Back to the present.

JANE. He seems harmless.
Do you think they're really on our trail?

JO. Look, word's getting out about the cause.

CATHY. But there's no way they could find us that fast.

A rustling.

ELIZABETH. Aw shit what was that?

CATHY. Girls! Grab your knives!

They all grab their knives. Lizzy throws her textbook open and grabs a knife sheathed inside the back cover.

JO. DO you think it's

CATHY. SHUT UP SHHHHHHH

A moment, they stand. Frozen. And then
River Sister emerges from the grasses.

JO. Who are you

RIVER SISTER. You didn't receive my ribbon?

ELIZABETH. No

RIVER SISTER. Well then we have to hurry
I may already be too late.

CATHY. Who ARE you?

RIVER SISTER. I'm St. John River's Sister

JANE. My pants!

He's the man whose pants I stole

High-fives all around.

CATHY. How did you find us, River Sister?

RIVER SISTER. I found a hanky in my brother's house
The very same brother who took you out of that gutter, strange woman
I now know your name is Jane Eyre
And you, Jo March
And you, Cathy Linton
And you, Liz Bennet
And almost as soon as I put the hanky down I dispatched my ribbon and set out to find you
To warn you that the men are coming
They are on their way
With maps and charts
They know that you are here
They know about you
On the moors
Now

JO. But how? How did they find us?

RIVER SISTER. The hanky mentioned somebody named Edgar Linton

CATHY. EDGAR LINTON?!

JANE. Should we run?

CATHY. I think we should stay and fight

ELIZABETH/JANE/JO. Fight?

JO. River Sister, what do you think we should do?

RIVER SISTER. If a battle is to be fought, then I know many women who would stand and fight with you
In fact.

She unveils a slew of ribbons from her cloak.

They're already on their way.

JO. My sisters would stand and fight with me

ELIZABETH. As would mine

CATHY. You guys I already told you I don't have any sisters and it's really starting to grate on me—

JANE. Yeah me too it's like borderline insensitive at this point

RIVER SISTER. No, Jane
You have me.
I shall stand as your sister
You stole my brother's pants
Which is a very sisterly thing to do

CATHY. Okay so I still don't have any sisters?

JO. You have us, Cathy

CATHY. I do?

ELIZABETH. Yeah.

JANE. Yeah.

CATHY. You guys.

A blast is heard.

RIVER SISTER. They're here.

Another blast.

JANE. What was that?
I mean, that sounded close

CATHY. Hush

Another blast.

JO. FUCK

ELIZABETH. Oh God is this happening now? Oh God this is happening

Darcy, Heathcliff, Laurie, and Rochester stand facing the girls' camp.
Rochester makes a megaphone with his hands.

ROCHESTER. Attention, Ladies

ELIZABETH. UGH did he just say Ladies?

JANE. I just—I can't with this voice

ROCHESTER. *(Face.)* We have searched the world far and wide for you—

JO. SHUT UP

LAURIE. YOU SHUT UP!

ROCHESTER. —and we have now found you out.

Show yourselves to us, or be forcibly removed from your hiding spots.

CATHY. THIS IS RIDICULOUS

HEATHCLIFF. Quit crying and stand up.

ELIZABETH. YOU WANNA SEE US?

LAURIE. Yeah!

JO. WOMEN. STAND TALL

ROCHESTER. MEN! SHOW YOUR RANKS!

LAURIE. And we couldn't have done it without our most important informant!

ALL THE MARCH GIRLS. Mother!
It can't be!

MRS. MARCH. SO it is, my daughters
So it is.
I'm afraid it is so
Mrs. March? A traitor?
Well you know what I am?
I'm a mother,
And a mother does know best
AND WHEN THE INCREDIBLY RICH NEIGHBOR BOY WANTS TO MARRY MY DAUGHTER
AND SHE REFUSES HIM AND RUNS OFF TO ANOTHER CITY AND LEAVES HER FAMILY SCROUNGING FOR MONEY AND FOOD
THEN WHAT? HUH? THEN WHAT IS Mrs. March SUPPOSED TO DO?
Morals don't feed kids, okay!
Morals don't cure ailments and dispositions, amiright BETH?
You girls think you're so "progressive" and "cutting edge"
For "following your dreams" and "forging your own path"
"independent women" don't eat S'MORES FOR DINNER
I found you out. I'm here. Fighting for the men
Because you've really rankled my garters, girls
And I'm ready to show you how to live a good woman's life

JO. I can eat s'mores.
I can eat s'mores whenever I WANT!

CATHY. They fight
The battle begins

PLAYER 1. It's just like *Game of Thrones,*

LAURIE. but also like capture the flag.

JANE and PLAYER 1. It's also like cops and robbers

PLAYER 5. But also like *The Karate Kid*

DARCY. But also like *Home Alone*

ELIZABETH. But also like basketball

HEATHCLIFF. But also like four square

ROCHESTER. But also like who can eat the popsicle the fastest

PLAYER 2. But also like *Nickelodeon GUTS*

PLAYER 4. But also like girls rule boys drool

PLAYER 6. But also like the first is the worst second the best the third the nerd with the hairy chest

PLAYER 5. But also like *Ninja Turtles*

ALL GIRLS. But also like *Star Wars*

ALL BOYS. But also like the *The Baby-Sitters Club*

ALL GIRLS. with knives

PLAYER 2. It is a surprise to Bingley that Caroline chose the girls' side

CATHY. It is a surprise to Cathy that Edgar was the one who snitched on the girls' whereabouts

ELIZABETH and DARCY. Bingley kills Caroline

JANE and ROCHESTER. AND/OR Jane exorcises Caroline from her body
And then, things get serious.

ALL BOYS. Jokes are made at the expense of slutty sisters

ALL GIRLS. Jokes are made at the expense of oversensitive men

JANE. Threats are made of the burning of houses

JO. The burning of stories

CATHY. The burning of grass and hair

PLAYER 2. Beth is killed in battle

ALL GIRLS. BEEEEEEEEEEEEEETH

JANE. Rochester's eyes get burned

ROCHESTER. MY EYEEEEEEES

PLAYER 6. St. John abandons and retreats to a ship bound for India

JANE and PLAYER 6. YOU'RE A COWARD, ST. JOHN. LET IT BE KNOWN

BINGLEY. And Then

ALL BUT CATHY. Cathy is stabbed.

Shock. Silence.

CATHY. Ow.
Goddammit.

HEATHCLIFF. Cathy?

CATHY. Hey. I hate you, right?

She falls into Heathcliff's arms.

HEATHCLIFF. Yeah you do. I hate you, too.

CATHY. Heathcliff.
Heathcliff, come here so I can whisper something

HEATHCLIFF. Okay?

Heathcliff puts his ear to her mouth.
She smiles
Stretches her arms
Yawns
And then
She dies.

Cathy?

JANE. but
but she was going to sail around the world

HEATHCLIFF. We don't want to play anymore.

All the women stare at him.

This wasn't how we thought it would turn out.

JO. How did you think it would turn out?

ALL GIRLS. How did you think it would turn out?

HEATHCLIFF. I don't know. Better than this.
Better than this.

ELIZABETH. Leave us.
All of you.

The men drop their weapons.
Dejected.
Without a word
They leave.

The women mourn Cathy.
Their friend
A life cut short too soon.
Then before they can allow themselves so much room for grief they gather themselves for their next uphill battle.

JANE. You mustn't be sorry for us

JO. You must be sorry for your own self
We must be sorry for our own selves

ELIZABETH. And sorry for no more than a minute

JO. And after that, we must continue to survive

ELIZABETH. It's hard to feel sorry for yourself and survive at the same time

JANE. And I daresay, no one will do either for us.

JANE, ELIZABETH, and JO. We must do it for ourselves.

They make a pact, with each other, that we will never hear.
They part ways.

End of Act Three

ACT FOUR
THE END OF THE BOOK

This act is to be staged with Cathy as main narrator, and each character saying their lines of dialogue as written. The 6 Players can play the museum workers in alternating fashion, as they wish.

Chapter 33
"Time heals all moors."
—River Sister

So they found themselves that evening at the Pemberley Museum, which made sense, since they worked there. Tonight, though, they were not tearing tickets ($7.50/Adult, $4.00/Student, Free/Children), or breaking into one of the empty galleries to play Where's Mrs. Rochester?, or leading special-exhibition tours ("The Clothes They Threw," "The Hankies They Sent"). No. Not tonight.

Tonight they found themselves polishing silver, stringing up balloons, stirring punch. One of the attendants stood precariously on a ladder, toes tipped, trying to pin the exclamation point on an overhanging sign that read: HAPPY 10 YEARS

Indeed, tonight marked ten years since the Armistice Treaty of Pemberley was signed. The Treaty hung on the wall in a newly Windexed and always-gilded frame, waiting impatiently for a glimpse of the faces of those who signed her long ago. Tonight, the War of the Moors would be honored with a reunion reception, a speech, and a toast. Many veterans would be enjoying the open bar, and an assortment of shitty canapés. They would probably not enjoy having to wear name tags, or seeing their fabled enemies of yore. For who enjoys seeing old lovers? And who can feign calling them friends?

A chime. A clock. Seven. Normally closing time. But not tonight. Tonight, Amy March-Laurence scrambled through the double doors of the ballroom. Her name tag read "AMY!" She offered to host tonight's affair at the museum in memory of her sister Beth. She winced as she ticked to-dos off her clipboard-list. Her heels were one size too small.

"Time check!" called Amy.

"It's almost time," replied the attendant who was nervously stirring punch.

"Great," said Amy. She walked over to the punch bowl, grabbed a plastic cup, and the Punch Bowl Attendant ladled out a gulp of punch. Amy tasted the gulp.

"Is this just a big margarita?"

"Yes," Punch Bowl Attendant said quietly.

"Great. Can we get some music on? I'm gonna be at check-in." Amy scampered out of the room, nearly eating shit at the doorway.

Nobody laughed. They liked their job too much to laugh.

The double doors closed behind her, and like clockwork, they could hear her welcoming someone in. The attendants dispersed to their various posts. Punch Bowl, DJ, canapés. Joseph stood next to the dimmers, in case he was called upon for a dramatic lighting change.

The doors opened. They held their breath

Mr. Darcy ambled in, wearing a name tag that said "DARCY." They all exhaled in relief.

"I am the…firstonehere!"

He strode around the room, high-fiving each of them them. Punch Bowl Attendant ladled him a fat cup and passed it to him. Darcy used to be their boss at the Museum, back when the Museum was still his house. When he traveled in town he'd stay in the corner of the house that was still cordoned off to visitors, where his sister Georgiana still lived. Some evenings they would find him after closing, wandering the halls, lingering in front of certain displays. But that was happening less and less. They were all very happy he came.

Almost immediately, the doors opened again. Laurie Laurence walked in. His name tag read "WORLD'S BEST BOOGERFACE." He wiggled this thumbs awkwardly and nodded at a few attendants. They smiled back

"Hey buddy!" said Laurie when he spotted Darcy. He walked over and put his hand out. Darcy shook it.

"Hey man!"

"It's been a long time."

"No shit. Hey!"

"Amy was so excited when you agreed to host."

"My pleasure. I mean, perfect venue."

"Perfect venue. Topical as fuck."

"Totally. Will Heathcliff be here?" Darcy asked.

"He never RSVPed," said Laurie.

"What a fuckhead."

"I know!"

A few seconds of silence went by. The two grown men just sort of stared quietly at each other. And then, Jo March walked in. Her name tag read "JOOOOOOOOOOOOOOOOOOO." Laurie couldn't suppress a little giggle.

"Hehe."

"Heh...hiiiii!" Jo got a little blushy and walked over.

Amy peeked her head in to watch her husband greet her sister. Sometimes she just wanted to squeeze both of them because she loved them so much.

"You guys!" she called, "I love you guys! Darcy! It looks so great in here!"

"Don't thank me! Thank all these guys," he said, gesturing to the attendants. They all blushed and smiled.

"Thanks guys! Okay, back to the door. Bye hun," Amy called to Laurie, and she left again.

"Hi," said Laurie.

"Hi," said Jo.

"It's been a long time," said Laurie.

"I mean I saw you at Christmas," said Jo. "Darcy—did you know Laurie married my sister?"

Darcy's eyes went wide as he remembered about fourteen conversations that made much more sense now.

"OHHHHHHHHHHHHHHHHHHHHHHH."

"Yeah!" said Jo, laughing.

"Yeah," said Laurie, a little proud and a little sheepish, "Amy!"

"Oh my God, Oh my God. Yes. Okay. Yes."

"What about you, Darcy?" Laurie asked. "Did you ever get married?"

Darcy's eyes got soft. The attendants held their breath and looked at each other. They knew he was experiencing one of The Twelve Emotions.

"Well... No. I...uh... No."

"Yeah, me either," Jo piped up. She could sense something was wrong. "War correspondents don't have much time for love."

"Oh right, you're doing that!" Darcy said, relieved to change the subject.

"Pulitzer Prize BITCH!" Jo moved to high-five the Punch Bowl Attendant, but he was in the middle of adding more triple sec to the bowl, so he missed it. Jo hoped nobody saw even though everybody did.

"Yeah, it's cool," she continued."Is this punch a boozy punch?"

"Yes," the attendant replies meekly. He ladles her a cup.

"Thank God," said Jo.

The door blew open and they all turned around to see Jane Eyre stumbling through it. Her name tag read "JANE." As soon as she got into the room, she fell to the floor. Jo rushed to her.

"Jane!! You okay?!"

"Yeah," Jane said, getting up. "Guys, I literally landed like four hours ago."

"From where?" asked Laurie.

"SPACE! I'm an astronaut now."

The attendants marveled. They'd met countless war heroes and political statesmen during their trips to the Pemberley Museum. They'd met TV celebrities and celebrity chefs. They had never encountered an astronaut.

"Herst fert qwork?"

They all looked at Jane. Did she make that sound? She was doing a weird thing to her own arm.

"Sorry, what?" asked Darcy.

"Nothing," said Jane, who was back to normal. "I got this weird PH thing implanted in my arm and sometimes it short-circuits. I meant to say, 'What are you up to?'"

Laurie started in. "Well, I work for a tech start up. It's pretty cool? I mean I'm just a portfolio manager. But yeah! We live outside of Boston. Me and Amy and our son Roscoe."

Jane turned to Darcy.

"What about you? Uhhhh, is there alcohol? I hate small talk so much."

"Weelllll." Darcy paused.

"He was in Parliament!" cried one of the attendants. They all looked at him, faces grave. Silence for a moment. Darcy held up a couple of fingers to the Punch Bowl Attendant, who rushed to ladle two new cups.

"You were in Parliament?!" asked Laurie.

"I lived in a posh and well-decorated flat in the heart of London," said Darcy. It seemed as though he was measuring his words. "I was popular with my constituents. I introduced several bills into law. I ran for prime minister. And I lost. Because the press did not think I was enough of a family man."

The Punch Bowl Attendant brought Darcy his cups. He handed one to Jane and cradled his own. And then, Lizzy Bennet came in.

Jo drags Jane toward Lizzy.

Name tag: Lizzy.

"Oh God," said Darcy. He took a swig. Mercifully, she was on her phone.

"Mom? Mom? Can I call you later? I just walked in. I know I told you I wasn't going. I left the lab early. We got the research grant—The research grant—THE GRANT. WE GOT IT. Thank you, Mom. No, I don't know who RSVPed. I'll tell you about it later. Call tomorrow. I promise. Okay byeeee," Lizzy hung up the phone. "My mom is fucking crazy."

The attendants had never met Lizzy Bennet, much less seen her and Mr. Darcy in a room together. In the Lovers' Debate exhibition room, there was an entire oak cabinet devoted to the two of them. It was the main attraction of the museum. Seeing them inhabiting the same room was too much. Darcy didn't know whether to take the secret passage in the wall behind the DJ to the conservatory, where he could water plants and gather thoughts and make a teary phone call to Paolo.

"You got the grant!" exclaimed Jo as she went to hug Lizzy.

"Fuck yeah I did!"

"You guys keep in touch?" Jane asked, a little jealous.

"We send letters sometimes," Jo said, sensing this.

"Jane," Lizzy said, "you've been in space for four years."

Jane conceded. "There's no letters in space"

Darcy slowly walked toward them. The others noticed this,

and they all made their way elsewhere to let them have their time. Jane took in some exhibits. Jo noticed the Treaty, hanging on the wall. Laurie eyed out the DJ's turntables and gave a thumbs up in approval.

"Hey," said Darcy to Lizzy.

"Oh! Hi," Lizzy replied. "Pemberley! This is your house!"

"Well you know, was my house. Now it's a museum about us." They both laughed to cover up the fact that they were all dying inside. Darcy recovered.

"What's the grant for?" he asked.

"Alzheimer's research," Lizzy said.

"Congrats."

"Thanks. Hey, um. So, I know what you did for my sisters."

"Oh!"

"Jane and Lydia. So…I just wanted to say thanks." Lizzy's eyes shifted to the floor. Darcy met them.

"No problem. Okay," Darcy said, ruffled. "I need more punch."

"Yeah," Lizzy replied, "I need more punch too."

"It's not really punch, it's like a big margarita."

"Sounds good."

Darcy took Lizzy's arm and started to lead her toward the punch. The attendants gasped, and suddenly Lizzy noticed how many people there were in the room.

"So where you going?" asked Darcy.

"To get some punch."

"No I mean after the reunion's over. Where are you staying?"

"Some inn. I'll probably head back to the city in the morning."

"Oh. Cool," said Darcy, thinking.

"What about you?"

"Well, my sister still lives in the North Wing of the house so I might spend the weekend here." Darcy said. "She's upstairs if you want to meet her. She really looks up to you guys (the women stuff)."

"Yeah," Lizzy said. "Yeah. Let's get some punch and then…go do that."

The attendants watched this all in shock. They expected cocktails thrown on dress shirts or teary mascara or letters delivered in a spiteful nod to the old days. But civil interaction? Friendly, even?

No Moors War scholar would have ever predicted this.

"What is going on?" asked Jo, who seemed to be thinking the same thing.

"I have no idea," replied Laurie. He seemed a little inspired by what he had just seen. He stood straight, with a steely resolve. "Hey."

"Yeah?"

"I read that book you wrote about us," Laurie said.

"Yeah?" Jo replied, queasy.

"It was good."

Jo was relieved.

"Shut up," she said.

Laurie smiled.

"You shut up."

They stood there, both of them happy as clams, for a long while. And then the double doors opened again. Rochester stood.

They noticed his killer sunglasses. His name tag read: ROCHEST. He reached his hand out, coolly, for a banister or a wall-moulding to guide him into the room. He stumbled a bit. Jane saw this and began ambling toward him. Her space legs continued to fail her. And she wobble-walked, and he wobble-walked, both knowing their purpose and not letting their bodies fail their minds' intentions. When they finally reached each other, they sort of fell into each other's arms and fell over. Part by accident, part not. It could have all been chalked up to being very space-legged or very blind. But they all knew it was something else.

Jane and Rochester hoisted each other up. "Jane."

"How could you tell?"

"Tiny hands."

"How's your wife."

"She died."

"Do you have a new one?"

"Miss Ingram! Miss Ingram! No I'm kidding. I have," he made a face, "no wife. And what's become of you? You're very wobbly."

"Space legs. I've been in space. By myself. You?"

"Well, I—I mean I don't even want to tell you. I hate small talk so much."

"Me too! I was just saying that to Darcy!"

"Okay well then can we cut to the emotional dramatic stuff

then? I'm just gonna do it. I don't have eyes anymore so the only images I have are the ones I've chosen to remember. And ten years later, the only thing I want to remember is you."

"Mr. Rochester, sir. There are thousands of memories that you can project onto the life you've lived. Some are true and some are not true. Did you know there's a display in this museum called *The Bean Varietals of Thornfield*?"

"I don't care about beans anymore, Jane."

"What about the ugly tree?"

"It was struck in half by lightning. It was torn apart."

"Mr. Rochester," Jane began. "I knew what I had to do, where I had to go. I did not question that where I was and what I did would every day be defined by my loneliness. I vowed that until the day I was fully satisfied with loneliness, I will never attempt duality. But now, I'm back from outer space, and—"

Jane kissed Rochester. He pulled away, surprised.

"Whoa," he said.

"Four years away from all humanity really makes you realize some things," Jane said.

"Jane. I'm sorry about all this."

"People shouldn't say sorry," Jane replied. "People should just ask for help when they need it. And you need some help getting to the punch, so I'm going to walk you to the punch."

"There's punch?" Rochester asked.

"There's a lot of punch."

Arm in arm, they fell toward the punch. The door opened, and they turned to see Professor Bhaer walk in. Nobody knew who he was except for Jo, who turned red, and one of the attendants, who was normally in charge of the espionage exhibit and knew everything about Bhaer's role as an informant to the women's side during the war.

"Hey guys! This is my date!" Jo yelled, a little too loudly!

"Hallo!" Bhaer waved.

"Hey," replied everyone.

"You look good," said Jo.

"Danke. Hey, so do you!"

"Danke."

Then Amy came back into the room. She held up her plastic cup and tried, with no success, clinking it to get the room's attention.

"Hey guys!" she called out. Everyone turned toward her.

"Thank you, everyone," Amy continued. "In case I didn't meet you at the door, my name is Amy March-Laurence. We're so excited to have nearly all of our veterans here tonight at the Pemberley Museum for the ten-year anniversary of the signing of the Armistice Treaty."

Everyone clapped. The attendants clapped hardest.

Amy continued, "We've come a long way since the battle was fought, and that's why tonight is so important. To speak a little more on that, ladies and gentlemen, I'm proud to present recent British Poet Laureate River Sister."

The attendants gasped. This was a surprise. Cheers erupted in the room as River Sister took the stage in her billowing cloaks. She was part Stevie Nicks, part Joni Mitchell. She was the most famous of them all.

"Thank you," River Sister began, quieting them all. "Thank you Amy. Thank you others. I would like to do a reading from my latest collection, which is dedicated as always to the memories of two people. The first is my brother, St. John Rivers. The second is departed General Cathy Linton Earnshaw."

The applause was sturdy, earnest.

"And now," River Sister said, "Time Heals All Moors."

Time is truly
On our side
In the years since we last met
Out on the grassy battlefields
Beyond time,
Beyond grass
Beyond hearts and passions dancing like firelight
There is an intention
It's over there
In words, in pages
Document-strewn
Focus! Now! O, there over there!
Do you see the thing you're looking for?

The rapt audience was bewitched by Rivers Sister's delivery.

They hardly noticed a towering man enter the room through the double doors. Unbeknownst to all of them, the man grabbed the Armistice Treaty off the wall and out of its frame. Out of his pocket he took a Zippo lighter.

No one noticed the burning until it was too late.

"OH!" River Sister yelled, and pointed to the back of the room. There stood Heathcliff, surrounded by ash and smoke, holding an empty gilded frame.

Amy March-Laurence screamed. The room descended into chaos.

Men put women behind them, Jane puts Rochester behind her.

One of the attendants marched toward Heathcliff, the rage of scholar and loss in his eyes. He swung a punch. Heathcliff dodged it and swiftly decked him with one move.

"Heathcliff!" cried Darcy, "What have you done?!!"

"What I wanna know is," Heathcliff said, "what would Cathy think about all this? Why would Cathy die for you people? What would Cathy do if she saw all of you drinking your stupid punch and trying to forget the miserable choices you made once?"

"Heathcliff, your damage is beyond repair," cried River Sister. "You're not welcome here."

A few attendants whimpered as Heathcliff moved toward River Sister. The others walked toward the ash on the floor, remembering what it once was.

"What did you say to me?" Heathcliff asked.

"I said you're not welcome here," River Sister said.

And then Heathcliff's knife came out. And as he readied himself to stab River Sister, a sharp "*SHHHHHHHH*" echoed through the room. Heathcliff stopped in his tracks. He looked around, knife in hand.

"Cathy?" he muttered.

And sure enough, there she was. Standing there, in the middle of the room, leg splayed to one side, scowl on her face. It was as though she had never left.

"Stop talking,"

"Cathy, is that you?"

"Stop talking to me. I'm dead."

"But Cathy!"

"Tell everyone to stop looking at me."

"Everybody! Stop looking at her!"

They all stared at him.

"Tell Amy to put on a good song. Tell them all to dance and make me jealous."

"Amy, put on a song. Everybody dance."

Amy apprehensively made her way toward the DJ booth and made a little signal. As soon as the song came on, the attendees and attendants made their way to the middle of the room. They began to slow-dance. It was quite tentative at first, but then each pair began to sink into their own separate worlds. Sameness and separateness in their dancing.

Darcy and Liz. Amy and Laurie. Jo and Bhaer. Jane and Rochester. River Sister and the ashes of the treaty. The attendants, arms around each other. Cathy spoke.

"Heathcliff."

"What."

"You have to stop stabbing people."

Heathcliff teared up. "But I wanna!"

"I'm dead," Cathy declared. "You won't get me back."

"Okay."

"Get your shit together. Start answering the phone when your friends call you. Stop hatching evil plots. Stop burning artifacts."

"But look at all of them," Heathcliff said, disgusted. "They're lying to themselves."

"Not anymore," Cathy said, envious as she watched them dance.

"You lied to yourself when you were alive. You married Edgar and you loved me."

Cathy turned sharply to him. "And if I could have gone back and changed one thing, it would have been that. But guess what? Time is time, and I am dead, and I am the dirt now, and my cells are the grass, and so there's nothing anybody can do to make me feel better."

"But how are you here," asked Heathcliff, "if you are the grass?"

Cathy took Heathcliff's hand in hers.

"Decay works in strange ways. My body, it is there. It is mud. Bones are dust. They are there on the moors now. Until the moors are upended by a volcanic eruption brought on by climate change and the explosion of faraway stars, and lava moves my materials toward a cliff on the edge of the sea, and I sink to the bottom, and form a cove for fish and anemones.

"But my spirit? My spirit is everywhere. It is here, now, with you, at this reunion, stroking your hair. And it is in France, legs dangling off the side of a canal, finishing up a bottle of wine. And it is in the jungles of the Amazon, blazing a trail down a whitewater river, using a branch of strange ivy to save Horchata, my mangy wild dog, from a patch of quicksand.

"It is around you and it is with you. And it is far away from you and it is not with you. My spirit cannot be in one place, and that is the wonderful sad thing of life, and of death. For we never know where we will be. And we always look for the place we will be. And we end up everywhere and nowhere, with no focus,

"Nothing fixed
And always moving toward
'Some
Where
Else.'"

Cathy kissed Heathcliff's forehead, and with that, she turned and walked away from him and then she was gone.

The men and women continued to dance. The Ten-Year Reunion of the signing of the Ashpile that once was an Armistice Treaty was coming to a close. Soon the halls of Pemberley would change from a party hall to a museum once again.

Heathcliff walked to one of the palatial windows and opened the curtain to see the stars. Sure enough, there she was. There, On The Moors of the sky. She danced. He did not smile. But still. It was something.

The End.

PROPERTY LIST

(Use this space to create props lists for your production)

SOUND EFFECTS

(Use this space to create sound effects lists for your production)

Dear reader,

Thank you for supporting playwrights by purchasing this acting edition! You may not know that Dramatists Play Service was founded, in 1936, by the Dramatists Guild and a number of prominent play agents to protect the rights and interests of playwrights. To this day, we are still a small company committed to our partnership with the Guild, and by proxy all playwrights, established and aspiring, working in the English language.

Because of our status as a small, independent publisher, we respectfully reiterate that this text may not be distributed or copied in any way, or uploaded to any file-sharing sites, including ones you might think are private. Photocopying or electronically distributing books means both DPS and the playwright are not paid for the work, and that ultimately hurts playwrights everywhere, as our profits are shared with the Guild.

We also hope you want to perform this play! Plays are wonderful to read, but even better when seen. If you are interested in performing or producing the play, please be aware that performance rights must be obtained through Dramatists Play Service. This is true for *any* public perfomance, even if no one is getting paid or admission is not being charged. Again, playwrights often make their sole living from performance royalties, so performing plays without paying the royalty is ultimately a loss for a real writer.

This acting edition is the **only approved text for performance**. There may be other editions of the play available for sale from other publishers, but DPS has worked closely with the playwright to ensure this published text reflects their desired text of all future productions. If you have purchased a revised edition (sometimes referred to as other types of editions, like "Broadway Edition," or "[Year] Edition"), that is the only edition you may use for performance, unless explicitly stated in writing by Dramatists Play Service.

Finally, this script cannot be changed without written permission from Dramatists Play Service. If a production intends to change the script in any way—including casting against the writer's intentions for characters, removing or changing "bad" words, or making other cuts however small—without permission, they are breaking the law. And, perhaps more importantly, changing an artist's work. Please don't do that!

We are thrilled that this play has made it into your hands. We hope you love it as much as we do, and thank you for helping us keep the American theater alive and vital.

Note on Songs/Recordings, Images, or Other Production Design Elements

Be advised that Dramatists Play Service, Inc., neither holds the rights to nor grants permission to use any songs, recordings, images, or other design elements mentioned in the play. It is the responsibility of the producing theater/organization to obtain permission of the copyright owner(s) for any such use. Additional royalty fees may apply for the right to use copyrighted materials.

For any songs/recordings, images, or other design elements mentioned in the play, works in the public domain may be substituted. It is the producing theater/organization's responsibility to ensure the substituted work is indeed in the public domain. Dramatists Play Service, Inc., cannot advise as to whether or not a song/arrangement/recording, image, or other design element is in the public domain.

NOTES

(Use this space to make notes for your production)